The MAILBOX
The Education Center

S0-BFD-459

Daily Math Prompts

One math prompt for every day of the school year!

- ## Review key math skills.

- ## Engage students in writing about math.

- ## Promote students' mathematical thinking.

Managing Editor: Gerri Primak

Editorial Team: Becky S. Andrews, Kimberley Bruck, Sharon Murphy, Debra Liverman, Diane Badden, Thad H. McLaurin, Lynn Drolet, Karen A. Brudnak, Juli Docimo Blair, Hope Rodgers, Dorothy C. McKinney, Sherry Hull, Margie Rogers

Production Team: Lori Z. Henry, Pam Crane, Rebecca Saunders, Chris Curry, Sarah Foreman, Theresa Lewis Goode, Greg D. Rieves, Eliseo De Jesus Santos II, Barry Slate, Donna K. Teal, Zane Williard, Tazmen Carlisle, Kathy Coop, Marsha Heim, Lynette Dickerson, Mark Rainey

www.themailbox.com

Manufactured in the United States
10 9 8 7 6 5 4 3 2 1

Table of Contents

How to Use This Book

Select a Prompt

To support your math curriculum, the prompts are arranged sequentially from easier to harder skills. Begin with the first page of prompts and work your way to the last page, or use the skills grid on page 4 to help you choose prompts that best suit the needs of your students. The handy checklist on page 77 will help you keep track of the prompts you've used throughout the year.

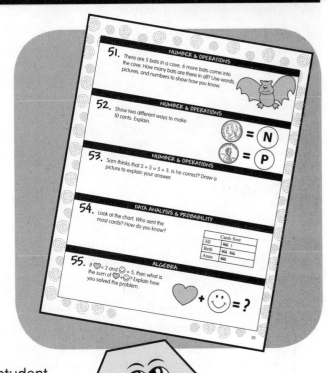

Display the Prompt

Prompts can be displayed in many ways. Here are a few suggestions:

- Photocopy selected prompts and cut them into strips. Give one copy of a selected strip to each student.

- Make copies of a page of prompts and give one to each student at the beginning of the week.

- Copy the prompt onto the board or on a piece of chart paper to display in the classroom or at a center.

- Make a transparency of the prompts to show on an overhead projector.

- If a visual is not needed, read the prompt aloud to students.

Additional Ways to Use This Book

- Use math prompts as
  - morning work
  - independent work
  - homework
  - a warm-up activity
  - a small-group activity

- Create individual student math journals by stapling a copy of the math journal cover (page 79) atop a supply of notebook paper. Or, if desired, use copies of the journal pages (page 80) instead of notebook paper. Math journals are a great way to keep a record of students' mathematical thinking and writing.

- Take a quick assessment of your students' mathematical thinking by using the assessment forms on page 78.

- Talk with individual students about their prompts to get a deeper insight into their mathematical thinking.

Skills Grid

Skill	Prompt
NUMBER & OPERATIONS	
Number Sense	
comparing numbers	111, 153, 157
comparing sets	2, 11, 17, 23, 31, 46
concept of zero	3
counting and reading numbers	28
counting by twos	48, 58
estimating	71, 161
even and odd numbers	73
making ten	8
number order	7, 12, 22, 33, 36, 42, 57, 81, 91, 143
one-to-one correspondence	1
ordinal positions	37
place value	83, 136, 147, 158, 168
problem solving	152, 156, 162, 173
Addition	
checking sums	67, 93, 122
commutative property	53
comparing sums	63
doubles facts	98
number line	61
story problems	6, 18, 26, 51, 62, 77, 88, 96, 106, 107, 117, 118, 121, 126, 127, 132, 141, 151, 167
two-column addition	176
writing a number sentence	66, 76, 116
Subtraction	
concept of subtraction	41, 101
story problems	13, 16, 21, 32, 43, 68, 78, 82, 87, 108, 123, 131, 133, 137, 146, 163, 172, 177
subtracting ten	102
Fact Families	
fact families	47, 56, 128
Money	
coin combinations	52, 97, 113, 148, 166, 178
coin values	38, 72
Fractions	
equal parts	92, 112
fair shares	27, 86, 103, 142
parts of a whole	138, 171

Skill	Prompt
GEOMETRY	
comparing plane and solid figures	90
plane shapes	10, 20, 30, 40, 50, 59, 99, 105, 135, 165
solid figures	65, 74, 114, 124, 155, 174
symmetry	144
MEASUREMENT	
calendar	35, 69, 125, 164
distance	160
length	5, 60, 120, 150
time	44, 75, 84, 95, 134, 179
weight	29, 104
width	14
DATA ANALYSIS & PROBABILITY	
bar graph	24, 79, 159
combinations	129
coordinates	180
picture graph	15, 39
pie chart	115
probability	9, 45, 70, 89, 109, 140, 170
tally chart	54
Venn diagram	100, 145
ALGEBRA	
missing addend	119
missing subtrahend	49
number patterns	64, 110, 169
patterning	4, 25, 34, 94, 130, 149
problem solving	85
sorting	19, 80, 139
using symbols	55, 154, 175

1. Cal the cat is wearing a sock on each paw. How many socks is he wearing? Tell how you solved the problem.

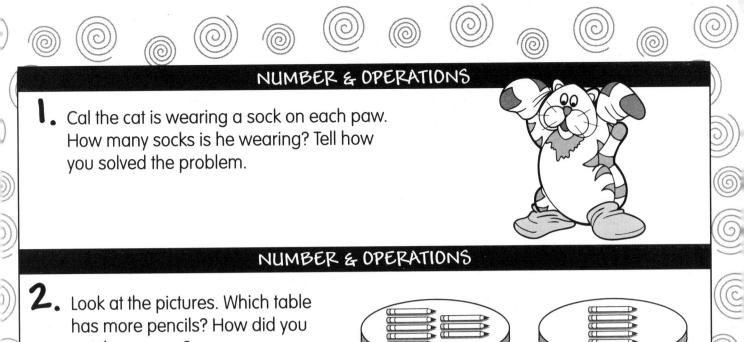

2. Look at the pictures. Which table has more pencils? How did you get the answer?

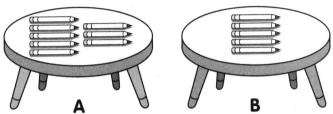

A   B

3. Lilly has 2 maps. Pam has 0 maps. How many more maps does Lilly have? Explain how you know.

ALGEBRA

4. Copy the pattern. Then draw the next three shapes. How did you know what to draw?

MEASUREMENT

5. Look at the pictures. Which snake is longer? How can you tell?

A

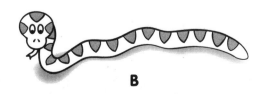
B

1. four socks

2. A

3. 2 maps

4. ○△○△○△○△○△

5. B

NUMBER & OPERATIONS

6. Jack has 3 bugs. Mack has 2 bugs. How many bugs do they have in all? Use pictures, words, or numbers to show how you know.

NUMBER & OPERATIONS

7. Copy and complete the list of numbers. How did you know what the missing numbers are?

1, ___, 3, 4, ___, 6, 7, ___, ___, 10

NUMBER & OPERATIONS

8. Look at the picture of the ten frame. How many more dots are needed to make a group of ten? Tell how you know.

DATA ANALYSIS & PROBABILITY

9. Kim has 2 black blocks and 8 white blocks in a bag. If she picks a block without looking, which color will she most likely pick? Explain.

GEOMETRY

10. Name the shapes shown. How are they the same? How are they different? Explain your answers.

6. 5 bugs

7. 1, 2, 3, 4, 5, 6, 7, 8, 9, 10

8. four dots

9. white

10. square, rectangle; Answers will vary.

NUMBER & OPERATIONS

11. Pat has 5 cookies. Draw a set that has more cookies. Explain your drawing.

NUMBER & OPERATIONS

12. Look at the pictures. Write the numbers in order from the least to the greatest. Tell how you know the order is correct.

NUMBER & OPERATIONS

13. Jill wants to read 4 pages in her book. She reads 3 pages. How many more pages does she need to read? Explain how you solved the problem.

MEASUREMENT

14. Look at the balloons. Which balloon is the widest? How do you know?

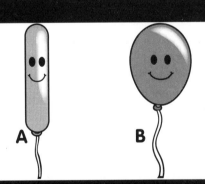

DATA ANALYSIS & PROBABILITY

15. Look at the graph. Does Jim have more red cars or blue cars? Explain your answer.

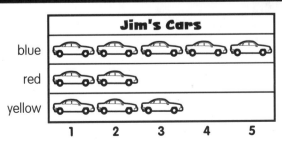

11. Answers will vary.

12. 11, 12, 13, 14, 15

13. 1 page

14. B

15. blue cars

16. Sally has 7 apples. How many more apples does she need to have 10? How did you solve the problem?

17. Look at the sets. Which sets are equal? Explain.

A

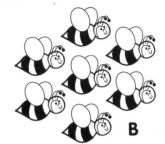

B

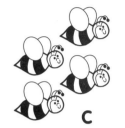

C

18. There are 2 dogs in the park. How many legs are there in all? Use pictures, numbers, or words to show your answer.

19. How could you sort these animals? Explain your thinking.

20. Which sign is not a square? Tell how you know.

A

B

C

16. 3 apples

17. A and C

18. 8 legs

19. Answers will vary.

20. A

©The Mailbox® • *Daily Math Prompts* • TEC61095

NUMBER & OPERATIONS

21. Joe is 7. Beth is 1 year younger than Joe. How old is Beth? How do you know?

NUMBER & OPERATIONS

22. Copy and complete the list of numbers. How did you know what the missing numbers are?

18, 17, ___, 15, 14, ___, ___, 11

NUMBER & OPERATIONS

23. Stan has 10 mints in a jar. Draw a jar with fewer mints. Explain your drawing.

DATA ANALYSIS & PROBABILITY

24. Look at the graph. Which two fruits are liked equally? How do you know?

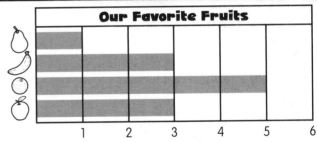

ALGEBRA

25. Show an **AABB** pattern. Explain your thinking.

_____ _____ _____ _____ _____

21. 6 years old

22. 18, 17, 16, 15, 14, 13, 12, 11

23. Answers will vary.

24.  and

25. Answers will vary.

NUMBER & OPERATIONS

26. Write a number sentence to explain this picture. How did you know what to write?

NUMBER & OPERATIONS

27. Betsy has 4 muffins. She wants to share them with Kia. How many muffins will each girl get if they share the muffins equally? Use pictures, numbers, or words to explain your answer.

NUMBER & OPERATIONS

28. Look. Which one does not belong? Explain how you know your answer is correct.

     three   **five**   **5**

MEASUREMENT

29. Which is heavier, the pencil or the glue? Explain how you know.

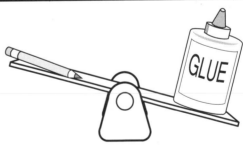

GEOMETRY

30. I am a plane shape with no sides and no corners. Draw my shape. How did you know which shape to draw?

26. 3 + 4 = 7

27. 2 muffins

28. three

29. glue

30. ◯

31. Which pan has more cookies?
How do you know?

A   B

32. There are 8 fish in the water. Then 4 fish swim away. How many fish are left? How did you get your answer?

33. Ann is thinking of a number. Her number comes before 10 but after 8. What is Ann's number? Explain your thinking.

34. Copy the pattern. Then draw the next three shapes. How did you know what to draw?

35. How many days are in the month shown? Tell how you know.

			October			
Sun.	Mon.	Tues.	Wed.	Thurs.	Fri.	Sat.
	1	2	3	4	5	6
7	8	9	10	11	12	13
14	15	16	17	18	19	20
21	22	23	24	25	26	27
28	29	30	31			

31. pan A

32. 4 fish

33. 9

34. △ ☐ ○ △ ☐ ○ <u>△</u> <u>☐</u> <u>○</u>

35. 31 days

NUMBER & OPERATIONS

36. Write these numbers in order from greatest to least. Tell how you know the order is correct.

21, 5, 10, 32, 16

NUMBER & OPERATIONS

37. Ducky is fifth in line. How many animals are in front of Ducky? Use pictures, words, and numbers to show how you know.

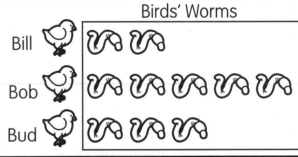

NUMBER & OPERATIONS

38. May has 2 nickels. Does she have enough money to buy gum that costs 10 cents? Explain.

DATA ANALYSIS & PROBABILITY

39. Look at the graph. Who caught the most worms? Who caught the fewest worms? How do you know?

Birds' Worms

Bill

Bob

Bud

GEOMETRY

40. Which set has fewer triangles in it? Explain your answer.

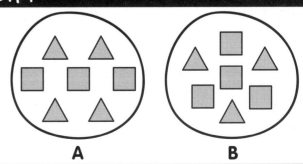

A   B

36. 32, 21, 16, 10, 5

37. 4 animals

38. yes

39. Bob caught the most. Bill caught the fewest.

40. set B

41. Draw a picture to illustrate the number sentence shown. Explain your picture.

$5 - 3 = 2$

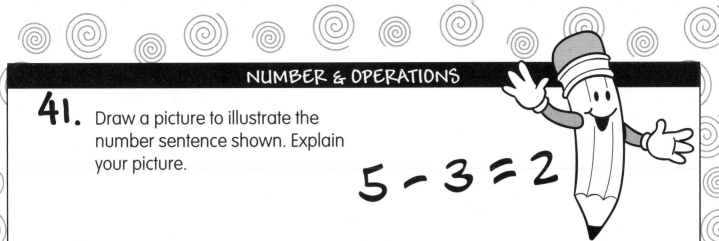

42. To count from 50 to 52, would you count forward 2 or count back 2? Tell how you know.

43. Mary has 8 flowers. Deb has 2 fewer flowers. How many flowers does Deb have? How did you solve the problem?

44. Stacy needs to be at school at 8:00. Which clock shows the correct time for her to be at school? How do you know?

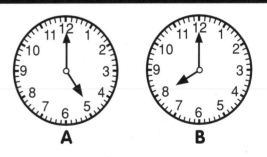

A   B

45. Is it possible or impossible that there will be purple cats in the sky tomorrow? Explain your thinking.

41. Answers will vary.

42. forward

43. 6 flowers

44. clock B

45. impossible

46. A mouse has a sock on each paw and 3 bells on its tail. Does the mouse have more socks or bells? Draw a picture to show how you know.

47. Look at the number sentences. All but one belongs to the same fact family. Which one does not belong? Explain.

$$6 + 2 = 8$$
$$2 + 6 = 8$$
$$8 + 2 = 10$$
$$8 - 2 = 6$$
$$8 - 6 = 2$$

48. Count the balls. How many balls did you count? Tell how you counted to solve the problem.

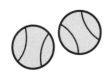    

49. What number makes this sentence true? How do you know your answer is correct?

$$6 - \underline{} = 5$$

50. Emma has a flat shape with four equal sides. Does she have a square or a triangle? How do you know?

46. socks

47. 8 + 2 = 10

48. 14 balls

49. 1

50. a square

51. There are 5 bats in a cave. 6 more bats come into the cave. How many bats are there in all? Use words, pictures, and numbers to show how you know.

52. Show two different ways to make 10 cents. Explain.

53. Sam thinks that 3 + 5 = 5 + 3. Is he correct? Draw a picture to explain your answer.

54. Look at the chart. Who sent the most cards? How do you know?

Cards Sent	
Jill	‖‖‖ l
Beth	‖‖‖ ‖‖‖
Anna	‖‖‖

55. If ♥ = 2 and ☺ = 5, then what is the sum of ♥ + ☺? Explain how you solved the problem.

51. 11 bats

52. Answers will vary.

53. yes

54. Beth

55. 7

NUMBER & OPERATIONS

56. Which fact is missing from this fact family? How do you know?

$$6 + 4 = 10$$
$$10 - 6 = 4$$
$$10 - 4 = 6$$

NUMBER & OPERATIONS

57. Write the number that comes before and the number that comes after 49. How did you know what to write?

NUMBER & OPERATIONS

58. There are 5 pairs of shoes in Carol's closet. How many shoes are there in all? How did you solve the problem?

GEOMETRY

59. How are these shapes alike? How are they different? Explain.

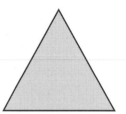

MEASUREMENT

60. Dan's pencil is 4 inches long. Tasha's pencil is 7 inches long. Whose pencil is longer? Draw a picture to show how you know.

56. 4 + 6 = 10

57. 48, 50

58. 10 shoes

59. Answers will vary.

60. Tasha's pencil

©The Mailbox® • *Daily Math Prompts* • TEC61095

NUMBER & OPERATIONS

61. I am the answer to the number sentence 6 + 2 = _____. What number am I? Use a number line to show your answer. Explain.

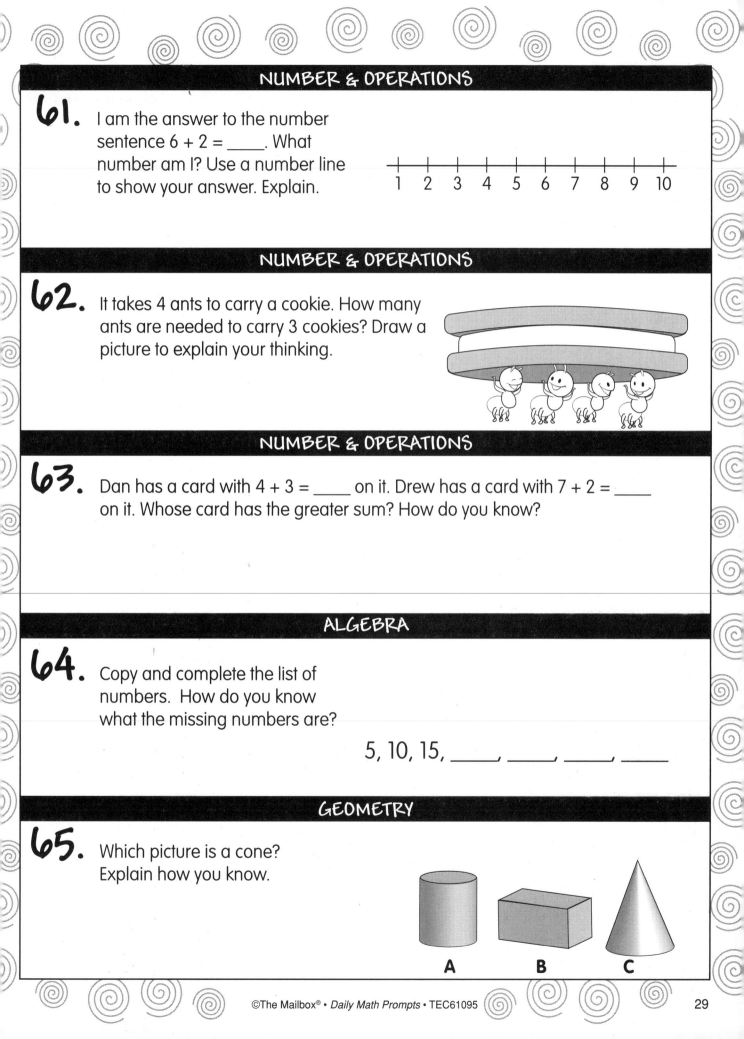

1 2 3 4 5 6 7 8 9 10

NUMBER & OPERATIONS

62. It takes 4 ants to carry a cookie. How many ants are needed to carry 3 cookies? Draw a picture to explain your thinking.

NUMBER & OPERATIONS

63. Dan has a card with 4 + 3 = _____ on it. Drew has a card with 7 + 2 = _____ on it. Whose card has the greater sum? How do you know?

ALGEBRA

64. Copy and complete the list of numbers. How do you know what the missing numbers are?

5, 10, 15, _____, _____, _____, _____

GEOMETRY

65. Which picture is a cone? Explain how you know.

A   B   C

61. 8

62. 12 ants

63. Drew

64. 5, 10, 15, 20, 25, 30, 35

65. picture C

66. Lee has a domino. Write a number sentence that shows how many total dots are on the domino. Explain.

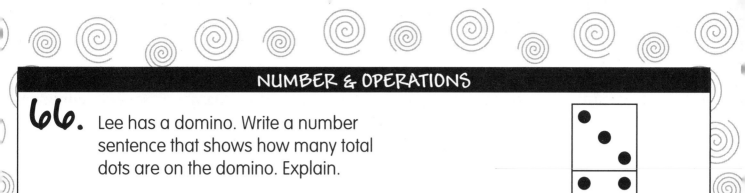

67. Tell whether the number 10 makes each sentence true. Tell how you know for each.

a. $5 + 5 =$

b. $6 + 3 =$

c. $3 + 7 =$

d. $4 + 6 =$

68. Reed has 7 stickers on his shirt. Then 5 stickers fall off. How many stickers are left? Use pictures, numbers, and words to show how you know.

69. Fred's birthday is in four days. If today's date is May 11, what is the date of his birthday? Explain your thinking.

🌞 🌞 🌞 May 🌞 🌞 🌞						
Sun.	Mon.	Tues.	Wed.	Thurs.	Fri.	Sat.
		1	2	3	4	5
6	7	8	9	10	11	12
13	14	15	16	17	18	19
20	21	22	23	24	25	26
27	28	29	30	31		

70. Dan has 10 green crayons and 2 red crayons in a box. He takes a crayon out of the box without looking. Which color is he more likely to pull out? How do you know?

66. 3 + 5 = 8 or 5 + 3 = 8

67.
a. yes
b. no
c. yes
d. yes

68. 2 stickers

69. May 15

70. green

NUMBER & OPERATIONS

71. Do you think there are 20 or 100 apples in the bag? Explain your estimate.

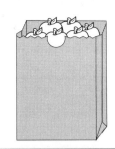

NUMBER & OPERATIONS

72. Jay has a dime. Rick has a quarter. Who has more money? How do you know?

NUMBER & OPERATIONS

73. Which number is an even number? Explain how you know.

$$3 \quad 17 \quad 11 \quad 8$$

GEOMETRY

74. Look in the classroom. List three things that are spheres. Tell how you know that your answers are correct.

MEASUREMENT

75. Jenna eats her snack at 11:00. Look at the clock. Is it time for Jenna to eat her snack? Explain your thinking.

71. 20 apples

72. Rick

73. 8

74. Answers will vary.

75. no

NUMBER & OPERATIONS

76. Write a number sentence with a sum of 7. Use pictures, numbers, and words to show your thinking.

NUMBER & OPERATIONS

77. Draw three groups of 5 apples. How many apples are there in all? Use your picture to explain.

NUMBER & OPERATIONS

78. Sarah's blue shirt has 6 buttons. Her red shirt has 4 buttons. How many more buttons are on her blue shirt than on her red shirt? How do you know?

DATA ANALYSIS & PROBABILITY

79. Each student in Mia's class voted for his or her favorite ice-pop flavor. Which flavor is liked the most by Mia's class? Which flavor is liked the least? Explain how you know.

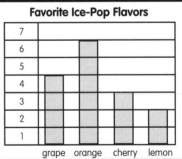

Favorite Ice-Pop Flavors

ALGEBRA

80. Draw the buttons, sorting them into groups in your picture. Use your drawing to explain how you sorted the buttons.

76. Answers will vary.

77. 15 apples

78. 2 buttons

79. orange, lemon

80. Answers will vary.

81. Look at the gifts. Write the numbers from largest to smallest. Explain how you know your answer is correct.

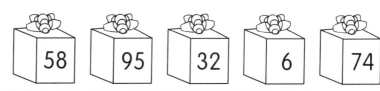

58 95 32 6 74

82. Amy has 9 books. If she gives 4 books to her friends, how many books will she have left? How did you solve the problem?

83. Mike has straws grouped into ones and tens. If he has 8 tens and 5 ones, how many straws does he have in all? How do you know?

84. Santos went to the park at 3:00. He played for 2 hours and then went home. What time was it then? How do you know what the time was?

85. Max, Lulu, and John are standing in line. Max is first. John is third. Where is Lulu? How do you know that your answer is correct?

81. 95, 74, 58, 32, 6

82. 5 books

83. 85 straws

84. 5:00

85. second in line

NUMBER & OPERATIONS

86. Bill and Sal share 6 gumdrops. If they each get the same number of gumdrops, how many will each get? Explain.

NUMBER & OPERATIONS

87. Pete has 4 pennies in one hand. If he has a total of 10 pennies in his hands, how many pennies is he holding in the other hand? How did you get your answer?

NUMBER & OPERATIONS

88. Ted had 3 pet turtles. His mom gave him 4 more turtles. The next day, his dad gave him 2 more turtles. How many turtles does he have now? Explain how you know your answer is correct.

DATA ANALYSIS & PROBABILITY

89. Mary has 10 blue fish, 2 yellow fish, and 4 silver fish. If she uses a net to catch a fish, which color fish is she most likely to catch? How do you know?

GEOMETRY

90. How are these two figures different from each other? Explain.

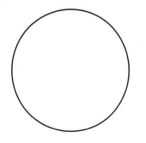 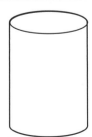

86. 3 gumdrops

87. 6 pennies

88. 9 turtles

89. blue

90. Answers will vary.

91. Copy and complete the list of numbers. How did you know what the missing numbers are?

10, 12, ___, 16, ___, 20

92. Look at the squares. Which one is divided into equal parts? How do you know?

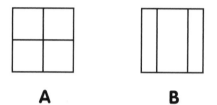

A   B

93. Is the number sentence 5 + 4 = 8 true or false? Explain.

94. Use letters to label the picture pattern. Explain how the letters match the picture pattern.

95. Jeff and Chloe started reading at the same time. If it took Jeff 5 minutes to finish his book and it took Chloe 5 hours to finish her book, who finished reading first? Tell how you know.

91. 10, 12, <u>14</u>, 16, <u>18</u>, 20

92. square A

93. false

94.
A B B A B B A

95. Jeff

96. There are 7 dogs. Each dog has 2 ears. How many ears are there in all? Draw a picture to show how you know.

97. Meg has a dime, a nickel, and three pennies in her pocket. She thinks she has 23 cents. Is she correct? Explain.

98. 3 + 3 = 6 is a doubles fact. Write three more doubles facts. Explain your thinking.

99. What is the total number of triangles in the design? Tell how you solved the problem.

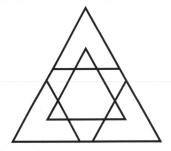

100. Look at the Venn diagram. If Jari wants to write the letter **B** on the diagram, where should he write it? Tell how you know.

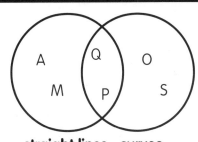

straight lines   curves

96. 14 ears

97. no

98. Answers will vary.

99. 8 triangles

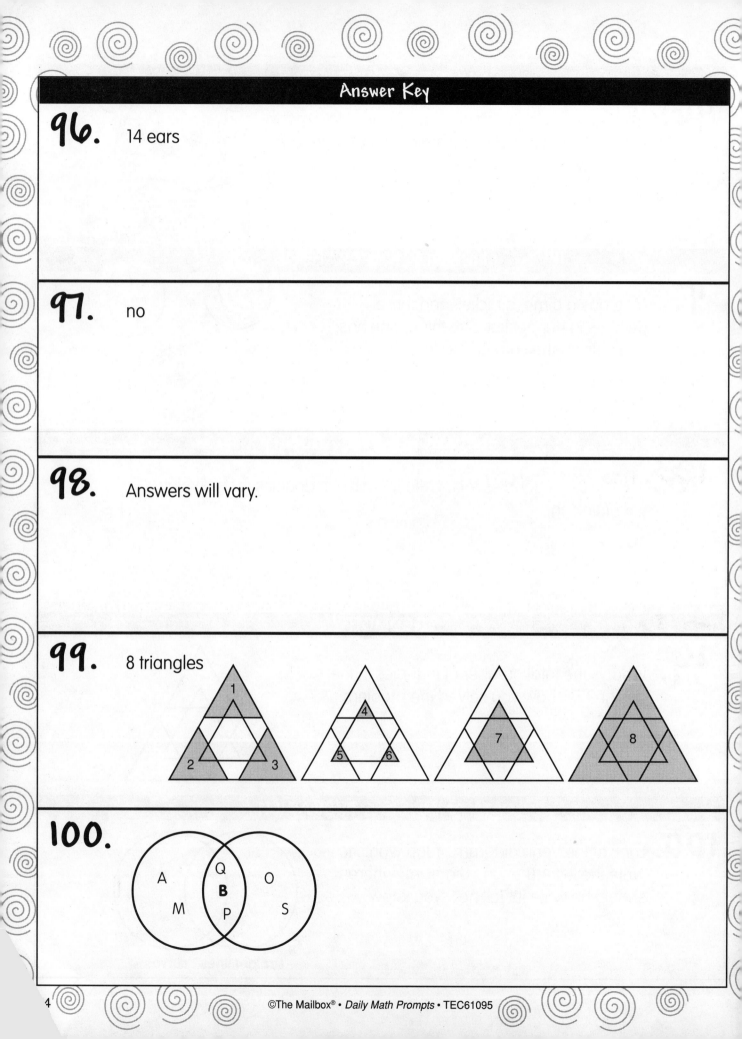

100.

101. Draw a picture that shows this number sentence. Explain.

$$12 - 4 = 8$$

102. What number is 10 less than 50? Tell how you solved the problem.

103. Fred, Gina, and Ed want to equally share 9 pretzels. How many pretzels will each child get? Draw a picture to explain your thinking.

104. Would you use a scale or a ruler to measure the weight of a pumpkin? Explain your choice.

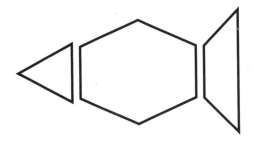

105. Name the shapes in this design. Tell what makes each shape different.

101. Answers will vary.

102. 40

103. 3 pretzels

104. a scale

105. triangle, hexagon, trapezoid

106. There are two bowls with marbles. If there are 7 marbles in each bowl, how many marbles are there in all? Explain your thinking.

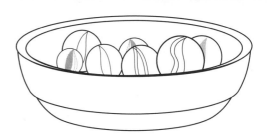

107. There are 8 girls and 7 boys in Mr. Finn's first-grade class. If Mr. Finn has 15 whistles, does he have enough whistles to keep one for himself and give one to each first grader? How do you know?

108. James has 12 crayons on his desk. 4 roll off. How many crayons are left on his desk? Did you add or subtract to solve the problem? Why?

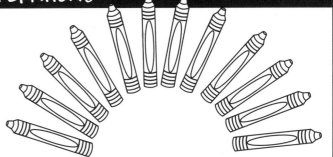

109. Ms. Jones put 10 black seeds and 4 yellow seeds in a bag. If she removes a seed from the bag without looking, is she more likely to get a black seed or a yellow seed?

110. Spencer read 10 pages on Monday, 20 pages on Tuesday, 30 pages on Wednesday, and 40 pages on Thursday. If the pattern continues, how many pages will he read on Friday?

Day	Mon.	Tues.	Wed.	Thurs.	Fri.
Pages read	10	20	30	40	

106. 14 marbles

107. no

108. 8 crayons, subtract

109. a black seed

110. 50 pages

111. Jan has 12 markers. Ken has 21 markers. Who has more? Tell how you know.

112. Frank divides his apple in half. How many equal pieces does he have? Explain.

113. Tom has 5 dimes. If gum costs 40 cents, does he have enough money to buy the gum? How do you know? Would he have any money left? If yes, how much? Explain.

114. How many cubes were used to make this figure? Use pictures or cubes to show how you know.

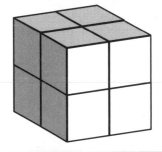

115. After a trip to the farm, the students in Mr. Moo's class voted for their favorite animals. Look at the graph. Which animal do most students like? How do you know?

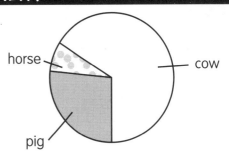

horse

cow

pig

111. Ken

112. 2 pieces

113. yes, 10 cents left

114. 8 cubes

115. cow

NUMBER & OPERATIONS

116. Here's one way to show 7. Think of at least three other ways to show 7. Use numbers, pictures, and words to show your answer.

$$2 + 2 + 2 + 1 = 7$$

NUMBER & OPERATIONS

117. There are 2 nests. If there are 4 eggs in each nest, how many eggs are there in all? How did you solve the problem?

NUMBER & OPERATIONS

118. Draw 20 **X**s in groups of five. How many groups are there? Use your drawing to show how you know.

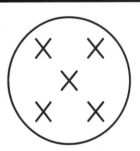

ALGEBRA

119. If $3 + \star = 9$, what is the value of $\star$? How did you solve for $\star$?

$$3 + \star = 9$$

MEASUREMENT

120. List six things in your classroom that are longer than your shoe. How do you know the things are longer?

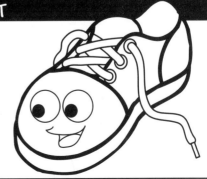

116. Answers will vary.

117. 8 eggs

118. four groups

119. 6

120. Answers will vary.

121. Alex has 16 grapes. Kay has 12 grapes. How many grapes do they have in all? Explain how you solved the problem.

122. David thinks $8 + 5 = 16$. Is he correct? Draw a picture to explain your answer.

123. It rained 3 inches on Monday and 7 inches on Tuesday. How many more inches did it rain on Tuesday than on Monday? How do you know?

124. Name the solid figures. Tell three ways that the figures are alike.

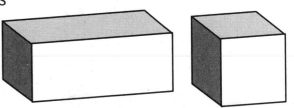

125. Emily went on a trip for 2 weeks. How many days did her trip last? How do you know?

April						
Sun.	Mon.	Tues.	Wed.	Thurs.	Fri.	Sat.
				1	2	3
4	5	6	7	8	9	10
11	12	13	14	15	16	17
18	19	20	21	22	23	24
25	26	27	28	29	30	

121. 28 grapes

122. no

123. 4 inches

124. rectangular prism, cube

125. 14 days

126. There are 9 pairs of mittens in a basket. How many mittens are there in all? Explain your thinking.

127. Kate, Bill, and Jeb picked apples. If they each picked 5 apples, how many apples did they pick all together? How did you solve the problem?

128. How does knowing that $9 + 5 = 14$ help you solve the following subtraction problem? Explain.

$$14 - 9 = \underline{}$$

129. Liz has a blue shirt, a red shirt, green shorts, and yellow shorts. How many different outfits can she wear? How did you get the answer?

130. Draw objects in an **AB** pattern. How did you know what to draw?

126. 18 mittens

127. 15 apples

128. Answers will vary.

129. 4 outfits

130. Answers will vary.

131. There are 14 boys and 8 girls in Mr. Burke's class. How many more boys are there than girls? How do you know?

132. Emma is making 4 dolls. She needs 2 buttons to make the eyes for each doll. How many buttons does she need in all? Draw a picture to explain your answer.

133. Tristan has 12 pencils. He found some more on the floor. Now he has 18 pencils. How many pencils did he find? Explain your thinking.

134. Bobby went to soccer practice. If practice lasted for 2 hours and he went home at 3:00, at what time did practice start? How did you get the answer?

135. Jackson cuts out 3 kites. If each kite has 6 sides, how many sides are there in all? How do you know?

131. 6 boys

132. 8 buttons

133. 6 pencils

134. 1:00

135. 18 sides

NUMBER & OPERATIONS

136. Write the largest possible number using the digits 5, 9, and 2. Then write the smallest number possible. Explain your answers.

NUMBER & OPERATIONS

137. There are 15 hot dogs. If Brittany eats 2 and Mark eats 4, how many hot dogs are left? Use pictures, words, and numbers to show how you know.

NUMBER & OPERATIONS

138. Rex cut a pie into 4 parts. He ate 3 parts. What fraction of the pie did he eat? What fraction of the pie was left? Explain.

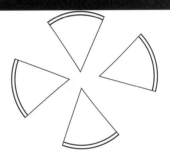

ALGEBRA

139. Jake has two boxes of stamps. He has a box for stamps that show animals and another for stamps that do not show animals. In which box would he store the stamp shown? Tell why you think so.

DATA ANALYSIS & PROBABILITY

140. The sun rises in the east every morning. Is it likely the sun will rise in the east tomorrow? Explain your thinking.

136. 952, 259

137. 9 hot dogs

138. ¾ of the pie, ¼ of the pie

139. the box for stamps that show animals

140. yes

141. Farmer Brown has 30 pigs. He gets 10 more pigs at the fair. How many pigs does he have now? Explain your thinking.

142. Kay has a dozen roses. If she shares them equally with her sister, how many roses will each girl get? Use pictures, numbers, and words to tell how you know.

143. Write these numbers in order from greatest to least. Tell how looking at the tens digit helps you put them in the correct order.

35, 82, 41, 29, 95

144. Does this shape show symmetry across the line shown? Why or why not?

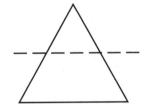

145. Look at the diagram. What kind(s) of ice cream does Sue like? Explain.

Favorite Ice Cream Flavors

141. 40 pigs

142. 6 roses

143. 95, 82, 41, 35, 29

144. no

145. chocolate and vanilla

©The Mailbox® • *Daily Math Prompts* • TEC61095

146. Molly has 14 chips. She hides 7 under a cup. How many chips are not hidden? Explain your thinking.

147. 40 bees can fit in the hive. If there are 47 bees, how many bees do not fit in the hive? Use ten frames to show you are correct.

148. Ray saved these coins in his piggy bank. Does he have enough money to buy a toy that costs 60 cents? Tell how you know.

149. Joy made a bead necklace. Her color pattern was green, blue, yellow. What color was the 7th bead? Use pictures, numbers, and words to show how you know.

150. Bob's flower is 18 inches tall. Kim's flower is 2 feet tall. Whose flower is taller? Explain how you know.

1 foot

146. 7 chips

147. 7 bees

148. yes

149. green

150. Kim's flower

NUMBER & OPERATIONS

151. Steve has 3 red bugs, 4 green bugs, and 5 purple bugs in a jar. How many bugs are there in all? Use pictures, words, and numbers to show how you know.

NUMBER & OPERATIONS

152. Ben has 2 jars that are the same size. He put 20 marbles in one jar. If he puts half as many marbles in the second jar, how many marbles will he have in all? Explain how you solved the problem.

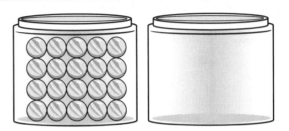

NUMBER & OPERATIONS

153. Fran sold 459 cards in the fall. She sold 491 cards in the spring. Did Fran sell more cards in the fall or in the spring? How do you know?

ALGEBRA

154. If 🚶 = 10 people and I = one person, how many people went to the fair? Explain your thinking.

People at the Fair

GEOMETRY

155. Look at the solid figures. Which figures can be stacked together? Name which figure must be on top. Tell why.

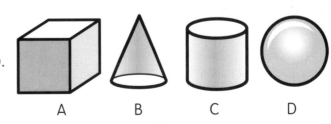

A   B   C   D

151. 12 bugs

152. 30 marbles

153. in the spring

154. 43 people

155. Figures A, B, and C; the cone

NUMBER & OPERATIONS

156. Maria has 30 socks in pairs. How many pairs of socks does she have? Use pictures, numbers, and words to show how you know.

NUMBER & OPERATIONS

157. Use >, <, or = to rewrite each statement. Explain how you knew which symbol to use for each.

29 is less than 87

56 is greater than 19

75 is equal to 75

NUMBER & OPERATIONS

158. I am a three-digit number. The digit in my hundreds place is 7. The digit in my tens place is 3 less than the digit in my hundreds place. The digit in my ones place is 1 more than the digit in my tens place. What number am I? Tell how you know.

_?_ _?_ _?_

DATA ANALYSIS & PROBABILITY

159. Look at the graph. Name the two colors that have the same number of marshmallows. How do you know?

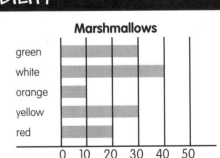

MEASUREMENT

160. Carly's grandma lives in the next town. If Carly wants to go for a visit, would it be faster for her to ride her bike or walk? Tell why you think so.

156. 15 pairs

157.
29 < 87
56 > 19
75 = 75

158. 745

159. green and yellow

160. It would be faster for her to ride her bike.

NUMBER & OPERATIONS

161. Danny sold 28 shirts. Neil sold 53 shirts. Tony sold more shirts than Danny but fewer than Neil. Which number could be the number of shirts Tony sold? How do you know?

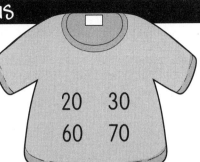

20   30
60   70

NUMBER & OPERATIONS

162. Jan has 43 eggs and 4 baskets. If she puts 10 eggs in each basket, how many eggs will be left over? Explain.

NUMBER & OPERATIONS

163. Karen caught 11 fish at the lake. If she took 3 fish home, how many did she let go? Draw a picture to show your thinking.

MEASUREMENT

164. Mandy is going to visit a friend in five days. If today is June 29, on what date will she visit her friend?

June						
Sun.	Mon.	Tues.	Wed.	Thurs.	Fri.	Sat.
					1	2
3	4	5	6	7	8	9
10	11	12	13	14	15	16
17	18	19	20	21	22	23
24	25	26	27	28	29	30

July						
Sun.	Mon.	Tues.	Wed.	Thurs.	Fri.	Sat.
1	2	3	4	5	6	7
8	9	10	11	12	13	14
15	16	17	18	19	20	21
22	23	24	25	26	27	28
29	30	31				

GEOMETRY

165. Name each type of shape used to make the robot. Draw your own robot using the same shapes. Tell about your drawing.

161. 30

162. 3 eggs

163. 8 fish

164. July 4

165. square, circle, triangle, rectangle, and oval

NUMBER & OPERATIONS

166. Abby has 4 dimes. Cole has 6 nickels. Who has more money? Explain how you know.

NUMBER & OPERATIONS

167. Liz went to the zoo. She saw 3 zebras, 14 monkeys, and 11 birds. How many animals did she see in all? How did you solve the problem?

NUMBER & OPERATIONS

168. Pete has some straws. If he has 3 sets of ten straws and 7 more straws, how many straws does he have in all? Use pictures to show how you know.

ALGEBRA

169. The rule for this pattern is to add 3. Write the numbers that complete the pattern. Tell how you know your numbers are correct.

1, 4, 7, 10, 13, ___, ___, ___

DATA ANALYSIS & PROBABILITY

170. Every time Kendra loses a tooth, a new one grows in its place. If she loses another tooth, is it likely that a new one will grow? Explain your thinking.

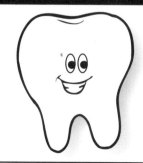

166. Abby

167. 28 animals

168. 37 straws

169. 1, 4, 7, 10, 13, 16, 19, 22

170. yes

NUMBER & OPERATIONS

171. Brad's pizza has 8 slices. He eats 3 slices and his sister eats 2 slices. What fraction of the pizza have they eaten all together? Use pictures, numbers, and words to show how you know.

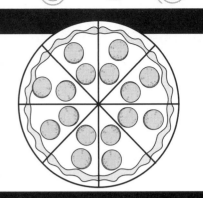

NUMBER & OPERATIONS

172. Nash has 24 tadpoles. If 13 tadpoles turned into frogs and hopped away, how many tadpoles would Nash have left? Write a subtraction problem to show your thinking.

NUMBER & OPERATIONS

173. Ms. Jones read 3 books a day to her class for a school week. How many books did she read in all? How did you solve the problem?

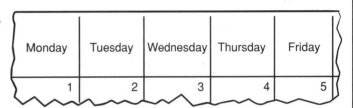

Monday	Tuesday	Wednesday	Thursday	Friday
1	2	3	4	5

GEOMETRY

174. I am a solid figure. All my sides are flat. Am I a cone, a cube, or a sphere? How do you know?

ALGEBRA

175. If △ = 4, what is the value of ☐? Explain your thinking.

$$\triangle + 3 = \square$$

171. $\frac{5}{8}$ of the pizza

172. 11 tadpoles; 24 – 13 = 11

173. 15 books

174. a cube

175. 7

NUMBER & OPERATIONS

176. Nan is solving the problem shown. She starts by adding 6 + 3. Is she correct? How do you know?

$$\begin{array}{r} 56 \\ + 31 \\ \hline \end{array}$$

NUMBER & OPERATIONS

177. Tess picks up 47 shells. She gives 23 shells to Pam. How many shells does she have left? Write a subtraction problem to show your thinking.

NUMBER & OPERATIONS

178. A sack of seeds costs 50 cents. Draw coins to show two ways to buy the seeds. Explain.

MEASUREMENT

179. It is 2:00 when Mom starts to clean the house. If she cleans for two and a half hours, at what time will she finish? Tell how you know.

DATA ANALYSIS & PROBABILITY

180. Mouse lost his strawberry. Name the coordinates where he can find it. How do you know your answer is correct?

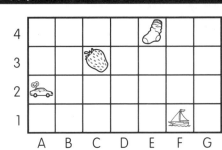

176. no

177. 24 shells; 47 − 23 = 24

178. Answers will vary.

179. 4:30

180. (C, 3)

Math Prompt Checklist

Use this handy checklist to help you keep track of each prompt used throughout the year.

✓	Prompt	✓	Prompt	✓	Prompt	✓	Prompt	✓	Prompt	✓	Prompt
	1		31		61		91		121		151
	2		32		62		92		122		152
	3		33		63		93		123		153
	4		34		64		94		124		154
	5		35		65		95		125		155
	6		36		66		96		126		156
	7		37		67		97		127		157
	8		38		68		98		128		158
	9		39		69		99		129		159
	10		40		70		100		130		160
	11		41		71		101		131		161
	12		42		72		102		132		162
	13		43		73		103		133		163
	14		44		74		104		134		164
	15		45		75		105		135		165
	16		46		76		106		136		166
	17		47		77		107		137		167
	18		48		78		108		138		168
	19		49		79		109		139		169
	20		50		80		110		140		170
	21		51		81		111		141		171
	22		52		82		112		142		172
	23		53		83		113		143		173
	24		54		84		114		144		174
	25		55		85		115		145		175
	26		56		86		116		146		176
	27		57		87		117		147		177
	28		58		88		118		148		178
	29		59		89		119		149		179
	30		60		90		120		150		180

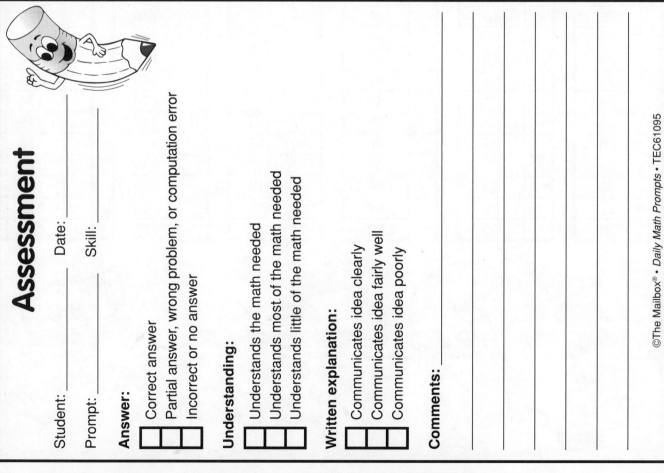

Assessment

Student: _____

Date: _____

Prompt: _____

Skill: _____

Answer:

☐ Correct answer
☐ Partial answer, wrong problem, or computation error
☐ Incorrect or no answer

Understanding:

☐ Understands the math needed
☐ Understands most of the math needed
☐ Understands little of the math needed

Comments:

Assessment

Student: _____

Date: _____

Prompt: _____

Skill: _____

Answer:

☐ Correct answer
☐ Partial answer, wrong problem, or computation error
☐ Incorrect or no answer

Understanding:

☐ Understands the math needed
☐ Understands most of the math needed
☐ Understands little of the math needed

Comments:

Assessment

Student: _____

Date: _____

Prompt: _____

Skill: _____

Answer:

☐ Correct answer
☐ Partial answer, wrong problem, or computation error
☐ Incorrect or no answer

Understanding:

☐ Understands the math needed
☐ Understands most of the math needed
☐ Understands little of the math needed

Written explanation:

☐ Communicates idea clearly
☐ Communicates idea fairly well
☐ Communicates idea poorly

Comments:

_____'s

Journal

$6 + 2 = 8$

Prompt Number: _____ Date: _____

Prompt Number: _____ Date: _____